MW01600550

IT PAYS TO BE SAVED

By

EVANGELIST
KAREN ANN THOMAS

Foreword by Apostle Claire Revealed

IT PAYS TO BE SAVED

BY

EVANGELIST
KAREN ANN THOMAS

CONTENTS

Dedication v

Acknowledgment vii

Foreword ix

Introduction xi

Chapter 1: Things you receive when you receive
          Jesus Christ...1

Chapter 2: Redemption from Darkness 5

Chapter 3: All Things New 9

Chapter 4: Bankrupt without God..................................13

Chapter 5: Jesus Christ the Gift of God.........................16

Chapter 6: Salvation Package for All.............................21

Chapter 7: How Do I Get Saved? 23

About the Author 26

DEDICATION

I would like to thank Father God for inspiring me to write this book, You could have written this book through anyone but You choose me, thank You for everything and thank You for creating me. Lord, I give You all the glory and the praise for this book; may lives be changed and souls brought back to You, thank You for Your word it is truth.

To Apostle Claire Revealed, just as there is no one like God, there is no one like you, you are unique. Thank you for being my spiritual mother, pushing back the darkness, and loving me enough to tell me the truth. May God raise up more people to carry such a fiery mantle as you do.

To Prophetess Yolanda Perry, thank you for your insight and prayers and time in the word.

To my Husband you are a great man of God! As I always tell you, you are a man with many mantles. May God prosper you and make you a great nation for His people.

DEDICATION

To my children and grandchildren, I love you all. Let the Lord

Be magnified in your life for all to see that God reigns I dedicate

This book to you all, Allow Jesus to be lord of your life and let the light of the gospel guide you into all truth.

To all Evangelist and soul winners around the world I dedicate this book to you!

ACKNOWLEDGMENT

I would not be the Evangelist that I am today, without the help of Pastor Darrell E White, thank you for your prayers, teaching, Leadership training, Minister training and Outreach training. Thank you for allowing mighty men and women of God to come in and train us and take us into the mission fields. Thank you for the emphasis you placed on how important it is to God that the Gospel of the Kingdom must be preached to all nations. Thank you Pastor Darcel White for investing your time and wisdom in me. I am grateful for you teaching me how to listen to what the Master is saying to me through His written word, and how each scripture has a work to do. Although it's been over 30 years, I am still impacted to this day by both of your teachings.

I would like to thank my loving, caring and supportive husband for allowing me time away from him; to write, inspire and encourage men everywhere to be saved. Thank you Honey!

I would also like to thank my parents who helped me, cared for me, corrected me, whooped me and loved me with all their heart; thanks Ma, thanks Daddy! God used you both to get me here, joining you together as one-unit, thanks for being my parents.

To my sisters and brothers, we had so much fun growing up and we are a force to be reckoned with. God has given us His love, no matter what life deals, when all is said and done; no condition, no drama, can tear us apart; we have so much to give and learn from each other. Thanks for helping me get to where I am on this journey. My prayer for you is that the light of God will shine in your lives, brighter than ever before, lighting the way for others to come to Christ Jesus.

Last but certainly not the least, to my children DeAndre, Rachael and my grandchildren Kayla and DeAndre Jr, I love you all.

FOREWORD

A true word from God is what we need in such a time as this! God is restoring foundations and one of the foundations being restored is the teaching anointing. In Jeremiah 3:15, God promised to give His people shepherds after His own heart, who will feed them with knowledge and understanding. You see, giving knowledge is passing on information, but passing on information without the ability to break it down so that the one receiving it can understand it, is useless. That is why I believe in this season God is raising up people like Evangelist Karen with the ability to teach, because teaching provides room for explanation and explanation brings understanding. Oh, how I pray that God would raise up more people who will not just give knowledge but also give understanding!

I also see the rising of the burning ones. These ones carry the heart of God and the passion of Christ. They understand that Jesus Christ came to seek and save the lost and they have made it their mission to see each soul turn to God and be saved. Evangelist Karen is one of the burning ones. Her one desire is to reach the world for God with the gospel of Jesus Christ. Not only does she want to see souls saved; she also wants to see them thrive in their walk with God. Karen is a woman who has seen the good, the bad and the ugly of life. She's been saved for many years and has walked with the Lord long enough to be qualified as one who can say, 'IT PAYS TO BE SAVED'.

I love this book because it carries a clear and powerful message for those who still need to be saved: for the backslider, the newcomers in Christ and for those who are in Christ but are doubting their choice to stay in God. I can also say this is a book for all of us, because we all need to be reminded that in Christ, we have all to gain and nothing to lose. There is such anointing of encouragement flowing through the pages of this book. I encourage every evangelist out there to get this book as it can also serve as a teaching manual.

May you begin to burn with fire and passion for Christ as you read this book. May you receive a deeper understanding of all that God has given to you through Christ Jesus and may you grow in Faith. May you become one that reconciles others to God as you are reconciled to Him. Amen.

Apostle Claire Revealed
Author of EVERY ESTHER NEEDS A MORDECAI
Founder of THE INTERNATIONAL GATHERING OF INTERCESSORS (Based in Holland)

INTRODUCTION

I was inspired to write this book when I realized that there are many Christians who are sons and daughters of the Most High God, living their lives without recognizing the benefit they have received in Jesus Christ from the moment they accept him as Lord and Savior. As heirs of salvation we are only going to be effective as soul winners, when we realize the benefits given to us by Christ Jesus.

This book is written as a tool to equip the saints for the work of ministry. Years ago, I went out evangelizing, getting people saved and bringing them into fellowship with other saints. Jesus Christ's heart is still beating and crying out, seeking to save the lost souls. The love of God is reaching out to those that are in trouble, reaching out to those that need a savior. As a result, this book is also written for those who don't know Christ, because God desires all men to be saved and come into the knowledge of truth.

I release this book for the use of generations of saints to come and for all those who would share the gospel of Christ with others, as the word declares: '**Wisdom is the principal thing; therefore get wisdom: and with all thy getting get understanding' Proverbs 4:7.** My prayer is that there will be an eye opening experience, so that the Spirit of understanding will rest upon everyone who is inspired to read this book, and may all who do so have an ear to hear what the Spirit of the Lord has to say to His Church in this hour.

May God unlock the wisdom in our hearts from his heart to win souls all around the world. The business of the kingdom must be preached to all men; may the church rise, take its place and be about the business of the impossible. For with God nothing shall be impossible **Matthew 19:25-26**. Arise and let this cry reach every heart, every region, every nation around the world; we can change the world by changing the way we think, let's begin to think like Christ. May God stir your heart into action and renew your love for Jesus, Amen.

CHAPTER ONE

Things you receive when you receive Jesus Christ

We receive so many benefits from God when we accept Jesus Christ into our lives, according to that which all His word produces in us and our lives. Brethren, it pays to be saved. Let me discuss with you a few of the benefits that you receive as a Child of God, a disciple of Christ Jesus:

The first thing we receive when we accept Christ in our life. is the Word of God.

John 1:1

In the beginning was the Word and the Word was with God.

We have been given the creative word of Christ which produces life in the believer's life.

According to **Ephesians 5:25-26** the *word is a cleanser*. Paul was encouraging husbands to love their wives, just as Christ

1

loves the Church and gave himself for her, that he might sanctify and cleanse her with the washing of water by the word. In **John 15:3** Jesus told his disciples **'Now you are clean through the word which I have spoken unto you,'** *the word of God will clean anyone who dares to come under its authority.*

We see through scripture, the powerful effect of having the word in our life; it can help us and save us from a lot of shame. The word instructs us on how to behave, it shows us the bad habits and behaviors we have, that need to be removed; some of these have been rooted deep down in our souls for generations.

Hebrews 4:12 declares that the word of God is quick and powerful, sharper than any two-edged sword. We have received the word of God that cuts both ways; it cuts and separates what is of the flesh and what is of the spirit. *The word of God exposes hidden thoughts and intentions that are embedded in our hearts* **Romans 12:2** - we have been given instructions to renew our mind with the word of God. His word *can renew our mind and give us New perspectives, New ideas, New things to enjoy, Renewed Strength, New Hope.*

God's word is alive, it speaks to our situation and our needs, it speaks to our pain and it encourages us in times of trouble. *God watches over His word to perform it in the lives of those who believe in Him.* **John 15:7** says , **'If you abide in me, and my words abide in you, you will ask what you desire and it shall be done for you,'** so because we follow the word of God we have *the benefit of asking God whatever we will and He will answer us according to His will,* because the word of God Abides in us.

This is how we become intimate with Jesus, giving our self to him, receiving him as our Lord, receiving his word, letting it be a part of our life and doing what he requires. Godly requirements are written to uplift and restore us back to his rest and peace. God's word will eliminate destruction, for Christ has redeemed us from the curse, having become a curse for the law, that we might become the righteousness of God in Christ Jesus, **Galatians 3:13-22.**

2 Corinthians 5:17 shows us that when we receive Christ, *we receive a new life*, old things are passed away and behold all thing become new - it pays to be saved! You start all over again, you become a new creation, you no longer need to be held back by your past because Christ has forgiven, saved, delivered and given you everything you will ever need. What a great gift!

2 Peter 1:3 says **'His divine power hath given us everything that pertains unto life and godliness, through the knowledge of him that hath called us to glory and virtue.'** *Everything has been given. All we need to do now, is to seek to know Jesus Christ with all our heart, will, mind and strength.* **Romans 8:31-32 (NKJV)** says **³¹'What then shall we say to these things? If God is for us, who can be against us? ³²He who did not spare his own son, but delivered him up for us all, how shall he not with Him also freely give us all things.'**

Romans 8:15-17 indicates that we *become the children of God*; what a benefit, we have been saved by the grace of God and God is a good father, he takes great care of his children. We are joint heirs with Jesus Christ, it pays to be saved! Now as you have received Christ keep your eyes looking towards him: **Hebrews 12:2.** He is the way, the truth, and the life: **John 14:6.**

James 1:19-25: *Jesus is our Life leader*, through the Holy Spirit he will guide you into all truth. As you show a willingness to get to know Jesus Christ through the word of God, you will begin to learn to know his voice. As you listen to his voice and follow his instructions not to be just a hearer, but a doer of the word.

God has given us all a measure of faith, so when you come to God, only believe that you will receive what you are desiring from God, and you will receive those things, as indicated in **Hebrews 11:6.** As you choose to lean into and trust in the Lord, you will learn more about the benefits you will receive from Christ. There is so much in the word of God. Making the decision to know Christ means you are on your way to a greater measure of wisdom, truth, revelation and love for Christ. Just knowing how Christ Jesus laid his life down for us, dying for us that we may be saved, already shows us his love and character.

I encourage you to journey with God, take his yoke upon you and learn everything about him. Know that as you receive him into your life, he is concerned about you, as it states in **Matthew 11:28,** calling you to come and *receive rest for your soul*, through the blood of Jesus Christ his Son.

CHAPTER 2

Redemption from Darkness

In **Romans 8:1-17 (NKJV)** it states, 'the Law of the spirit of life in Christ Jesus has made you free from the law of sin and death.' Christ has come to liberate us, to acquit us and to set us free from sin's grip, *sin can no longer have a hold on us.* **Romans 6:14 (NIV): 'For sin shall no longer be your master, because you are not under the law but under grace.'** Just think about that, sin can no longer control or govern our standards. Sin can no longer dictate to you, because you are under the law of grace which gives us life and peace, and frees us from the law of sin and death. So we are free, no longer bound, we have received redemption.

I felt so special when I learned that I was bought back for a high price and that I now belong to Christ. Knowing all the lengths he went to make me free and get me back, it was awesome. I was bound by sin and dead works, but I received Christ in my life, and so the journey began. I needed to understand about Christ and needed to learn what was expected of me, and to know how I fit in following what I had received.

5

Knowing the truth became very important to me, because we live in a world where there are many different opinions, facts and lies. I am in awe that God would have the bible written by men who were inspired by the Holy Spirit, the Spirit of truth; so that I would know the true cause of Jesus Christ's death. If Christ did not die for us, there would not be remission of sins.

Matthew 26:26-28 states communion is necessary, Christ died so that we can be

forgiven, and the stain of our sin washed away. I thank God for the blood, it works; it sanctifies us and unites us back to the Father. The blood of Jesus must be applied to our life for us to benefit from it, just like if your hands are dirty and you do not use soap to wash them, they will not be effectively cleansed. We must apply the blood of Jesus to our life situations, apply it to our mind and conscience, *to bring sanctification, cleansing and healing to our life*; Christ died to redeem us. That's good news - it pays to have Jesus in our life, he has been given to us by the Father for that very purpose, his blood has purposed it.

Colossians 1:19-20 says 'For it pleased the Father that in him should all fullness dwell; ^{20}And, having made peace through the blood of his cross, by him to reconcile all things unto himself; by him, I say, whether they be things in earth, or things in heaven.'

Hebrews 9:13-19 (NLT) Under the old system, the blood of goats and bulls, and the ashes of a heifer could cleanse people's bodies from ceremonial impurity. ^{14}Just think how much more the blood of Christ will purify our consciences from sinful

6

deeds, so that we can worship the living God. For by the power of the eternal Spirit, Christ offered himself to God as a perfect sacrifice for our sins. [15]That is why he is the one who mediates a new covenant between God and people, so that all who are called can receive the eternal inheritance God has promised them. For Christ died to set them free from the penalty of the sins they had committed under that first covenant. [16]Now when someone leaves a will, it is necessary to prove that the person who made it is dead. [17]The will goes into effect only after the person's death. While the person who made it is still alive, the will cannot be put into effect. [18]That is why even the first covenant was put into effect with the blood of an animal. [19]For after Moses had read each of God's commandments to all the people, he took the blood of calves and goats, along with water, and sprinkled both the book of God's law and all the people, using hyssop branches and scarlet wool.

The word says, 'Christ has redeemed us from the curse of the law of the land by becoming a curse for us, for it is written cursed is everyone who is hung on a tree,' Galatians 3:13 (NIV). In other words, Christ has bought us back, he died a horrible death for our salvation, you have been bought for a high price. Never allow anyone to devalue you, God the father knows the value He places on us, because of Jesus' sacrifice.

If you have received Jesus in your life never forget, you were purchased at a high price, **1 Corinthians 7:23.** Because of his payment *we received freedom from sin, from every curse and* *sickness there can ever be*; it pays to be saved. When you receive Christ into your life, you are *receiving forgiveness, you are receiving a stamp of approval on your life free from penalties and sins.* You are *receiving freedom from all debt notification* through adoption, being a son and joint heir of Christ's birth certificate; what the law could not do, God did by sending his son. **John 3:16.**

For the scripture says **'But as many as received him, to them gave he power to become the sons of God, even to them that believe on his name,' John 1:12.** That is good news that *we are joint heirs in the family of God*; it pays to be saved. We are no longer in debt to the flesh, neither do we need to live according to the flesh, for if we live according to the flesh we die, *but if we live by the spirit we put to death the deeds of the flesh*, **Romans 8: 12-17**. It pays to be saved.

We have *received the right to become sons of God, which allows us to inherit the sonship of Christ. When you receive Jesus and are led by the Spirit of God, you become an heir, then a joint heir with Christ.* That's Good News! Why not decide to give your life to Christ today?

CHAPTER 3

All Things New

When I received Christ, I was so excited at being given another chance. I was saved, single and wanted to please God. I found out that God had a plan for me and the plans I had previously envisioned for myself were not going to work, as they were totally against God's will for me. I learned that I had to think differently and the more I spent time with God, the more I learned about myself; my relationship with God deepened, He unveiled and unlocked my potential.

I learned to see myself through the eyes of Christ. At first, I was looking at myself through the eyes of the world and seeing its expectation of me; seeing myself the way family and friends saw me or I looked at myself in light of the things I went through in the past. Then after a while, I realized I was not the same person I used to be. Sometimes family and friends don't recognize right away the new you. It's not our job to prove to them that we have changed, our commitment is to prove ourself to Christ.

This new person I had become loved God to the extreme. I loved to sing about him, I would make up new songs about Him, I would praise Him no matter what. I desired to be with God more than I enjoyed doing anything else. I realized that God was with me; He loved me, He had invested in me, redeemed me, cared for me, provided for me consistently without fail, and always expressed His love for me.

Some of the people who knew me before, talked about me, making fun of me; however, I had experienced the love of God, and I knew that He wanted to highlight some things in my life that I would previously hide or shy away from. So, God placed in my spirit to lift Him up, singing new songs, the song of the Lord; just making a joyful noise unto the Lord, and I overcame! Now I love myself, and all that God has placed in me I use, to give Him glory and honor. Praise to His name! I always want to bring God in on the scene no matter what I am doing. It truly pays to be saved, *God himself will show you who you are, and you will come to love yourself.*

As you trust and rely on God to be your source, He will be the *source of wisdom, knowledge and revelation for you, for he will become your confidence,* Christ has redeemed us from the curse of the Law of the land, **Galatians 3:13**. As you receive him, *he will deliver you from the power of darkness and translate you into the kingdom of his dear son* because of his love: **Colossians 1:13**. It pays to be saved and have Christ our risen savior as our guiding light, for without God you can't do anything, as the scripture says.

In **John 15: 5 (NKJV)** Jesus says **'I am the vine you are the branches. He who abides in me and I in him, bears much fruit; for without Me you can do nothing.'** With God we can

10

be fruitful, powerful, loving, caring and enabled to do great things because we abide in Him, we become effective, fruitful and we bring this to our heavenly Father. When we pray and ask for anything in Jesus' name according to His will He gives it to us because we abide in him: **2 Corinthians 5:17** therefore if anyone is in Christ the new creation has come: the old has gone, the new is here!

The moment you decide to receive Jesus in your life, that is the moment you become a new creation in Christ. All things become new, as we read, hear, understand and meditate on the word we begin to renew our mind. We perceive the way God intends us to be, when we renew our mind with the word of God.

God has chosen us to let the former things go, so that we can enjoy our new life, in **Isaiah 43:18-19 (NIV)** He asks us to forget the former things: ...**do not dwell on the past, see I am doing a new thing, now it springs up**..., when we receive Christ we also receive a new identity, we become son and daughters of Christ.

John 1:12 (NLT) says **'But to all who believed him and accepted him he gave the right to become children of God.'**

So spiritually you receive a death and birth certificate at the same time: the scripture says old things pass away, behold all things become new.

2 Corinthians 5: 15-21 since old things have passed away, we no longer live by the same laws; under the old laws we live for ourselves, under the new law we live for Christ, our citizenship is of heaven we have to train ourselves to live in heavenly places where the law of the flesh becomes undone.

You no longer live indulging your carnal flesh, you must renew the spirit of your mind with the word of God, **Romans 8:6-16:** to be carnally minded is death, but to be spiritually minded is life and peace. In order to be a son or daughter of Christ you must make up your mind that you want all that was promised to you. The promise that you are now an heir of Christ; the promise that grants you a connection to his son.

To get this, you must choose to serve God with all your heart, with all your mind, and with all your strength, you must make a decision to yield your old way of thinking up to Christ, surrender your old way of doing things up to him. Then ask the Father to show you His way; show you how to live, how to walk in His way, tell Him, you are new to this. I would have grown so much quicker if someone had told me back then what I am saying to you now.

Don't try to figure out what to do, just ask the Holy Spirit to show you the way.

If old things have passed away, that means there is new way of doing things; even when you pray, give your old way of thinking to God. Ask God to give you His thoughts: *'in all your ways acknowledge him and he will direct your path' Proverbs 3:6 (NKJV).*

CHAPTER 4

Bankrupt without God

A life without Christ, what a tragedy, no one to free us from sins or curses. Without Christ we can do nothing, we will become like a branch that withers because it is not connected to the vine which is Jesus Christ. Jesus Christ is the source of life, the true vine in which we bear godly fruit, fruit that shall remain **John 15: 1–8**. Without Christ we are bankrupt, we are branches which must choose to abide in Christ.

Abide means: 1. to consent to be in contact with, and 2.to remain in fellowship with - to hang out together, lasting to stay, to dwell and endure.

Imagine this, Jesus is asking us to hang out with him. Without abiding in the vine that is Christ we can't bear fruit. It pays to be saved and be in fellowship with Christ. Consider inviting Christ in your life today - **Romans 8:1-2 (NKJV) says 'There is therefore no condemnation to those who are in Christ Jesus, who do not walk according to the flesh, but according to the Spirit. For the law of the Spirit of life in Christ Jesus has made me free from the law of sin**

13

and death. *Without Jesus you cannot be forgiven your sins.* No one to have mercy upon you, no one to guide you into the truth. The world is full of darkness, loads of bad advice and lies to keep you from the truth. But God so loved the world that He gave His only begotten son, to save a lost and dying world, **John 3:16**.

For all those that are born again or those that will make a decision to receive Jesus Christ who died for all; he bled so that you would be freed from every curse and sin, his blood was payment for us to enter into the kingdom of God. He paid a high price; saving us from all penalties of sin and death, **1 Corinthians 7:23.** So, I encourage you to choose life, choose Christ, for he died a terrible death just to capture us with his love and kindness, to draw us back into the light. The glorious light of the gospel that is full of grace and truth.

With God all things are possible: let me share this testimony with you. I was unwell and had six uterine tumors; I needed to be healed. Every morning my husband would ask God to shrink and remove the tumors. At the time, I believed God could heal any situation, as I had prayed to God to heal other people and he did. However, when it came to me needing healing, I struggled with believing God could heal me without surgery. As we both kept praying, asking that God shrink and remove the tumors, I began to trust and believe that God could do it for me.

I went to the Doctor, and she showed me and my husband the x-rays of the tumors: two of them were very large, but four of them not as large, so we kept on praying, asking God to shrink and remove the tumors. In April 2017, I went in for the surgery, but when I came out my husband said the

Doctor had informed him that she had looked and looked but could not find any of the tumors. I was amazed and kept on seeking God concerning this miracle. I asked, 'Lord, what did you do, what should I tell people that want to know what you did?' I was led to go to **Isaiah 53:5:** the Lord told me, 'I took it, I took it!' in a forceful voice. I screamed and shouted so loud, that I know I was heard miles away. He took away my infirmities, pain and sorrow just like His word said He would, and this changed my life forever and caused my faith to be at an all-time high. I believe *only God can do the impossible, if you dare to believe,* it really pays to be saved and believe God.

For with God nothing is impossible. Having a relationship with God makes all things possible, because Christ connects us with the things we desire and believe. We walk in faith, believing and trusting that God is willing and able to do what He said that He would do for us; there is no partiality in our God at all:
Romans 2:11-16.

God is our healer, our shield, our buckler, our strong tower, our provider; there is nothing too difficult or too hard for God. Surely His goodness can reach us at our point of need, surely God will deliver us from every obstacle that is in our way, as **Psalm 46:1** says **'God is our refuge and strength, a very present help in trouble**.' No matter what you are going through right now, *God will not leave you alone* - this is awesome, and it pays to be saved. You have a God that *will be with you in trouble and is willing and able to guide you into safety.* This safety is provided to all who are willing to accept Jesus Christ as their personal Lord and savior.

CHAPTER 5

Jesus Christ the Gift of God

This message is to the church, we cannot seek the lost with our own desires being more important in our heart and mind; deciding who we choose to pick, if they are wealthy, or if they have a job or based upon their background; Christ died for us all. In **Philippians 2:1-18** we are told to put on the mind of Christ, in other words we must follow Christ's way of thinking, looking out for the interests of others as well as our own. Like-minded means that as servants of Christ, we should be of one accord: having the same love and the same mission. For us to be effective as an Evangelist, Pastor, Teacher, Apostle, Prophet, or as a member of the body of believers doing the will and commission of Christ, we must have the mind of Christ.

The second thing we must do is put on the Lord Jesus Christ, **Romans 13:11-14**. We are here on earth to make a difference and to be a light to those who are in the darkness. It's time for us to awake and cloth ourselves in Christ. We are the light of the world, if we keep hiding our light or acting like the world, the lost will never come into the knowledge of Christ. They will never have an encounter with Christ, their blood and sin will be upon us and we will be held accountable.

Lastly, putting on Jesus will activate us to function in Jesus' mandate. The heart of Christ is still longing and seeking to save those that are lost: **Luke 19:1-10.** We must carry that same mandate in our heart to seek and save those that are hurt, lost, abused, discouraged, suicidal, those that are ready to throw in the towel, those that are sick and all those that are in need of Jesus in their life. It is time for us to search our hearts; Jesus specifically asked us to go and preach the Gospel to the lost, even if it means going into their homes, or jails, we need to go to the lost no matter where they are. Let them know that the kingdom of heaven is at hand, God is in the business of repairing lives, changing destinies, healing broken hearts and healing the sick.

The rebellious do what they will, however He is in the business of doing the impossible, the miraculous and making dreams a reality. His shed blood was what He paid to give you eternal life, so that all of mankind can be reconciled back to God. **Luke 14:23** says **"…Go out into the highways and hedges, and compel them to come in, that my house may be filled."** Disciples must make the most of every opportunity and preach the good news of the gospel to all nations, so that they can hear the gospel, **Matthew 24:14.**

He is saying, you are my disciple now GO into the world with the Gospel, seek and save the lost; we are the body of Christ, as Jesus is, so must we be in the world,

17

1 John 4:17. We must spread the love of Jesus, this is how love is perfected among us. Jesus commanded us to love one another **'By this everyone will know that you are my disciples, if you love one another,' John 13:34-35 (NIV).** We are called to share the love of God, so we must do our part by sharing the good news to all people, we must gather, clean and build them up for the work of the ministry as disciples of Jesus.

This process must be done in a demonstration of power: the lost need to have a love encounter, and experience the love and goodness of God and the care, concern, and fellowship of Jesus the son; this process is carried out by the Holy Spirit that dwells in us. We are His ambassadors on the earth sent out to express the love of Christ to the lost; with the Holy Spirit helping us, the anointing of God teaches us and confirms all things with signs and wonders following us. So, as we go out to heal the sick, they will be healed, demons will be cast out and we will baptize in the name of Father, Son and the Holy Spirit: this is the work that we must do.

We are in this world to proclaim the Kingdom of God and to lift the name of Jesus up on the earth, so that God will draw all men unto Jesus. If the gospel is hidden, it will be hidden from those that are lost. We have a great work to do, we must prepare the way of the Lord for those that are lost, that they may know Christ and the power of his resurrection. **1 John 2:20-27** tells us, you have *received an anointing from the Holy One* and you know all things. The Holy Spirit is the teacher, He is our guide and will lead us into all truth, He is going to give us instructions on how to cast our net and where to reach the lost.

There are many more things that we receive when we accept Jesus Christ as our Lord and savior; let me list a few in addition to those listed before:

We receive salvation, the gift of life, and the right to become a son or daughter of God, **John 1:12**

We receive the promise that God will never leave us nor forsake us, He will never abandon us, **Hebrews 13:5**

We receive eternal life through Jesus Christ, **John 3:16**

We receive Jesus Christ who is full of grace and truth, **John 1:14**

We receive every spiritual blessing in the heavenly realms, **Ephesians 1:1-6**

We receive the mercy of God, even when we were dead in our sins and trespasses. We have been saved by Grace, **Ephesians 2:4-10**

We receive a new family, different from that which we were born into, God is our Father and we have sisters and brothers, we are no longer lonely, **Psalm 68:5-6.**

There is so much more that we receive when we receive Jesus Christ in our life, *we receive a wealth of knowledge, his wisdom, his strength, and health that is released though the blood of Jesus, because we have his DNA.*
We have his desire in us that all men be saved and come into the knowledge of the Father through Jesus Christ our Lord.
We receive the greatest gift of all, that is God's love, and we are empowered to share it. The scriptures instruct us to '**owe no man anything, but to love one another...' Romans 13:8,** we must share the good news of the gospel in love, and go about doing good, we must give love, kindness, care and have mercy.

In closing this chapter, I want to leave you with this thought, Jesus said to his disciples as he sent them out, **'Heal the sick, raise the dead, cleanse those who have leprosy, drive out demons. Freely you have received, freely give' :Matthew 10: 5-8 (NIV).** We must go out to seek and save the lost souls, so they will know that God cares about their condition and the salvation of their souls. We have yet a lot of work, a lot of giving and a lot of producing to do in the Kingdom of God. It's our time to spread the love of Christ.

I have been trained several times in evangelism by great men and women through the years. We have led many souls to Christ through door to door ministry, nursing home ministry, tent revivals, and helping hands ministry. In one of the churches where I was a member, I headed the outreach ministry, I had to budget and plan the strategies for our outreaches: planning which neighborhood in our city we were going to evangelize, deciding if tent revivals suited the area, organizing praise teams, dance teams and getting an administrator to make sure the plans were executed.

God will give you wisdom on how to reach each region. We gave out in each area: groceries, food, bus tickets to get to work, Prayer Ministry and much more. I had an outreach team called Living in Faith Evangelism, so named because you must live in faith in order to fulfill the call of an evangelist. You must also have a heart for souls, a heart to help people, you must be selfless, and be willing to give of yourself. God will grace you with His power to tell others about His wonderful son, Jesus Christ. We must be willing to take every opportunity to share Christ with others, and eliminate all excuses, because we have received the greatest gift of Jesus Christ to share with others.

CHAPTER 6

Salvation Package for All

Within the salvation package is a lifetime of benefits that will never expire. God has promised us eternal life through the death of his son: **John 3:16.** Jesus died to give you eternal life, scripture tells us in **1 John 1:5:** whosoever has the son has life. Jesus' blood was poured out for our sins, for our infirmities, for all sickness and diseases. It was poured out to redeem us from poverty, poured out to connect us to his truth and righteousness, poured out to reconcile all things back to him, **Colossians 1: 19-20**. His blood has been poured out to redeem us from every curse and the law of the land. Jesus became a curse for us, so that the blessing of Abraham will come on us as we receive it though faith: **Galatians 3:13**.

Through the blood there is sanctification, nearly everything is cleansed by the blood of Jesus. Without the shedding of blood there will be no forgiveness of sins, **Hebrews 9:22,** so we all need Jesus to be our Lord and Savior. We need the presence of Jesus, for the son of God was manifested to destroy the works of the devil, we must invite Him into our life to connect us with the covenant blessings: it pays to be saved.

Without Jesus there would be no deliverance, no restoration, no redemption, because he purchased us for a high price with his precious blood; I am so glad that he died for our salvation. He died that we may be free from the passed-down sins of generations, the passed-down negative attitudes of our heart and mind. I am so glad that when God looks at us, He sees His son in us. Just because you have accepted Jesus Christ as Lord, does not mean you do not need him anymore. You need to hear his voice, you need to hold on to his promises. To understand what you have received, you need to become intimate with him.

Please receive Jesus Christ today, there are so many benefits we receive in Christ I have spoken of some of them in this book, and my prayer is you will allow Jesus to be the Lord of your life and discover the endless supply of benefits that our heavenly Father has in store for you. Allow Jesus to connect you to all his precious promises, allow him into your heart, to seal you in his blood, to justify you; allow Christ to restore you, deliver you and make you whole. In Jesus mighty name Amen!!!

CHAPTER 7

HOW DO I GET SAVED?

You are one decision away from making the most valuable decision of your lifetime, if you are yet to receive Jesus Christ into your life. This is a life changing moment for you right now! You must confess the Lord Jesus with your mouth, and if you believe in your heart that God has raised Jesus from the dead, you shall be saved, right now! **For with the heart one believes unto righteousness and with the mouth confession is made into salvation, Romans 10:8-10 (NKJV).**

Salvation is activated through our belief and confession that God has raised Jesus from the dead.

PRAYER FOR SALVATION

Lord Jesus, I believe that you are the son of God, I believe in my heart that God raised you from the dead, come into my life and be my Lord and my savior, I receive you right now, old things have passed away and all things have become new, in Jesus Name, Amen.

23

<u>If you prayed this prayer, welcome to the family of God!</u>

I Received Christ on………. (Date)

_____

Make sure you stay connected to Jesus, reading your bible, going to a bible teaching church, submitting to your pastor and church leadership so you can continue to grow in Jesus Christ.

This book was written to inspire those that have already received Christ, and for those that will come into the knowledge of the truth. This book will help you capture the heart of God and His love for the people that He created, most especially for those who will yield their life to Him.

In this book you will discover the benefits to be received when you accept Jesus Christ. To be truly effective as saints of Christ, we need to know the benefits we receive from accepting Christ and to know his mandate for us on the earth. This book is for those who desire to know Christ and to be in relationship with him, 'It Pays To Be Saved' and to know the love of Christ.

About the Author

Evangelist Karen Ann Thomas is hungry for God and focused on doing His will and fulfilling His purpose in her life. This passion began at a young age when she accepted Jesus Christ in New Friendly Missionary Baptist Church. A lifetime calling was born out of a song she sang in the youth choir, 'I want to be a Witness for Him, witness, witness, I am going to be a witness for Him'.

Married with children, evangelism is her lifestyle, and for years she has been ministering to the lost, praying for the sick, visiting nursing homes, youth jails, women's centers and shelters. As she had won so many souls who had no place to be churched, she started a cell group in her house. There she taught the word of God, feeding the families and administering the love of God to them, training disciples for the Kingdom. The cell group has now grown into a church, Karen Ann Thomas Ministries, which she currently pastors with her husband who is the Overseer.

Made in the USA
Columbia, SC
27 May 2023

17409320R00022